DATE DUE

Bodden, Valerie.

BIO   **Hillary Rodham Clinton**
CLI   **: historic leader**

Essential Lives

HILLARY RODHAM CLINTON

Essential Lives

HILLARY RODHAM
CLINTON
HISTORIC LEADER

by Valerie Bodden

Content Consultant:
Marianne Githens, Distinguished Professor of Political Science and
Chair of Women's Studies, Goucher College, Baltimore, Maryland

ABDO
Publishing Company

CREDITS

Published by ABDO Publishing Company, 8000 West 78th Street, Edina, Minnesota 55439. Copyright © 2010 by Abdo Consulting Group, Inc. International copyrights reserved in all countries. No part of this book may be reproduced in any form without written permission from the publisher. The Essential Library™ is a trademark and logo of ABDO Publishing Company.

Printed in the United States.

 PRINTED ON RECYCLED PAPER

Editor: Holly Saari
Copy Editor: Paula Lewis
Interior Design and Production: Emily Love
Cover Design: Emily Love

Library of Congress Cataloging-in-Publication Data
Bodden, Valerie.
  Hillary Rodham Clinton : historic leader / by Valerie Bodden.
      p. cm. — (Essential lives)
  Includes bibliographical references and index.
  ISBN 978-1-60453-699-7
 1. Clinton, Hillary Rodham—Juvenile literature. 2. Presidents' spouses—United States—Biography—Juvenile literature. 3. Women legislators—United States—Biography—Juvenile literature. 4. United States. Congress. Senate—Biography—Juvenile literature. 5. Women presidential candidates—United States—Biography— Juvenile literature. 6. Women cabinet officers—United States— Biography—Juvenile literature. I. Title.

  E887.C55B63 2010
  973.929092--dc22
  [B]
                          2009009984

Hillary Rodham Clinton

TABLE OF CONTENTS

Hillary Clinton with President Barack Obama
on her first full day as secretary of state

First for a First Lady

On January 15, 2009, the U.S. Senate Foreign Relations Committee recommended Hillary Rodham Clinton's nomination as secretary of state to the Senate. The Senate approved the appointment with a 94–2 vote.

Senator Clinton had just become the U.S. secretary of state.

The historical significance of this moment was profound. After a heated race for the Democratic presidential nomination, many wondered if Hillary could take a backseat to President-elect Barack Obama, who had been her political opponent for more than a year. Others wondered if the personal and political controversies she had experienced in the past would affect her role as liaison with the global community. Still others hoped Hillary's nomination would lead the United States from a warring nation to a more diplomatic one.

But what did Hillary plan to do in her new role? How would she approach other nations, and what tone would she set? Hillary answered those questions herself during the coming months as she addressed fellow foreign affairs officials:

Secretary of State

The secretary of state is the head of the U.S. State Department, which oversees U.S. foreign policy. The secretary advises the president on foreign affairs and directs the State Department to carry out the president's instructions in regard to foreign relations. State Department duties include enforcing immigration laws, directing military policy, assisting foreign governments, investigating international human rights abuses, and arranging visits with foreign dignitaries.

Hillary with Afghan President Hamid Karzaia, left, and Pakistani President Asif Ali Zardari, right, at the State Department in May 2009

I see [the work of the State Department] as really based on principled and pragmatic partnerships. . . . We've engaged emerging nations and pivotal regional actors on issues of common concern, from climate change and energy, to democracy and good governance, and regional and global security. We know very well that the work we've done so far to strengthen our relationships throughout this hemisphere and around the world are just a beginning. We don't have any illusions about how challenging the environment is that we are navigating. But we are encouraged by the positive responses that we have received to date.[1]

In the first few months as secretary of state, Hillary traveled to numerous countries, speaking with their leaders and discussing the challenges and opportunities they faced. She worked to promote the United States' policies and to strengthen ties with foreign nations. Hillary spoke on matters ranging from human rights to nuclear weapons and war.

In March 2009, a CNN/Opinion Research Corp. poll showed that U.S. citizens were happy with her job performance. Hillary's approval rating was at 71 percent, ten points higher than that of her predecessor, Condoleezza Rice, after a similar length of time in the position. It seemed Hillary's conflict-ridden past would not get in the way of her work with the State Department.

Going against Convention

With her appointment as secretary of state, Hillary Clinton became the only former First Lady to be nominated to one of the highest-ranking

---

Hillary's Books

Hillary has written a number of books, including:
- *Living History* (2003)
- *An Invitation to the White House: At Home with History* (2000)
- *Dear Socks, Dear Buddy: Kids' Letters to the First Pets* (1998)
- *It Takes a Village: And Other Lessons Children Teach Us* (1996)

diplomatic positions in the country. This was not the only time Hillary had been the first to achieve something.

In 1976, Hillary entered the public spotlight when her husband, Bill Clinton, was elected attorney general of Arkansas. Almost from that time, she had gone against convention. She served as a lawyer in Little Rock, Arkansas, at a time when the city had few female lawyers. Later, when Bill was elected governor of the state, Hillary took a leading role in helping reform the Arkansas education system.

When her husband became U.S. president in 1993, Hillary took on a more active role in policy making than previous First Ladies had done. She was the first wife of a president to have her office in the West Wing. This area is the location of the president's Oval Office and is considered the center of power in the White House. In 2000, Hillary was elected as a U.S. senator for New York, becoming the only former First Lady to serve in Congress. Only seven years after her election to the U.S. Senate, Hillary announced her intention to run for president—and she came closer than any other woman in history to securing a major party's nomination.

However, these firsts did not always make Hillary popular with the public or with her colleagues. Although some people admired her as the ultimate working mother, others accused her of being cold and inauthentic. While many women looked to her as an inspiration, some condemned her for moving outside of the traditional role of a First Lady. The widely differing opinions about Hillary were reflected in a 2006 *Time* magazine survey. The opinions led writer Ana Marie Cox to conclude that, although popular, the former First

Women in Politics

As has been the case throughout U.S. history, women today fill a minority of elected positions in the country. When Hillary Clinton was elected to the Senate, she became 1 of 13 women serving in the 100-member legislative body. The November 2008 election set a new record. Seventeen women were voted into the Senate. As of the 2008 election, the U.S. House of Representatives included 73 congresswomen out of 435 members. Across the country, more than 1,791 women were state legislators, and eight women were governors.

In a number of other countries, the percentage of women serving in politics is higher than in the United States. Norway, Sweden, Finland, and Iceland have high percentages of female representatives. Some countries have quotas requiring that a specific number of candidates for political office be women or that a certain number of legislative positions be filled by women. Among countries with quotas are France, Spain, Korea, Rwanda, and Afghanistan. While the United States has never had a woman commander in chief, Germany, Liberia, Chile, Israel, India, and Great Britain have all had women in their highest executive offices.

Lady might have been "the most polarizing figure on the current political landscape."[2]

A Life of Public Service

Hillary knew she wanted to be involved in public service when she heard the Reverend Martin Luther King Jr. speak in Chicago in 1961. By the late 2000s, she had spent nearly four decades serving the public in a variety of forums. As a law student at Yale, Hillary joined the fight for children and family rights. As First Lady, she spoke out for human rights around the world and attempted to reform the health care system in the United States. She continued working for these issues as a U.S. senator. Hillary expressed her lifelong commitment to serving after her defeat in the 2008 Democratic presidential primary:

> *I have an old-fashioned conviction: that public service is about helping people solve their problems and live their dreams. I've had every opportunity and blessing in my own life, and I want the same for all Americans. Until that day comes, you will always find me on the front lines of democracy—fighting for the future.*[3]

Hillary holding a news conference at the U.S. State Department in 2009

Hillary grew up in Park Ridge, Illinois. She often hung out at Pickwick Restaurant and Pickwick Theatre.

AN EARLY LOVE
OF POLITICS

Hugh and Dorothy Rodham were married in 1942. Hugh had served as a chief petty officer in the U.S. Navy during World War II. He was stationed at the Great Lakes Naval Station north of Chicago, where he trained sailors headed for fighting in the Pacific. After the war, he opened his own drapery business and later started a screen-printing company.

Hillary Diane Rodham was born in Chicago, Illinois, on October 26, 1947. Her brother Hugh was born in 1950, and her brother Tony was born in 1954. Their mother, Dorothy, stayed home to take care of the children.

Hillary's father had grown up in Scranton, Pennsylvania, and he remained close to his family there. Hillary and her brothers were baptized in the same Methodist church that their father had attended as a child. Every summer, the family visited Hugh's parents and siblings at the cottage he had built with his father on nearby Lake Winola.

Moving to the Suburbs

When Hillary was born, the Rodhams lived in a tiny one-

Hillary's Mother

When Dorothy Rodham was eight years old, her parents divorced. She and her younger sister were sent to California to live with their grandparents. The two girls rode the train from Chicago to the West Coast alone. In California, they found a harsh and unloving grandmother and a grandfather who ignored them. For nearly an entire year, the grandmother forced Dorothy to remain in her room when not in school.

When Dorothy was 14, she became a live-in babysitter for another family. The family's kindness showed Dorothy what it meant to have a loving home, and she followed their example when she had her own children.

bedroom apartment in downtown Chicago. By the time she was three, they could afford to move into a two-story house in Park Ridge. This suburb was a largely white, conservative community of middle-class professionals. Its population was approximately 16,500 when Hillary and her family arrived, but it doubled in size within ten years.

Hillary's neighborhood was full of children. She and her brothers spent much of their time running from one friend's house to another, playing softball, kickball, and tag. Throughout her childhood, Hillary was known as a tomboy. Though she was not always the best athlete in the game, her father had taught her enough football and baseball to make her a competent player. As she got older, Hillary also took to organizing neighborhood activities such as backyard carnivals and a mock Olympics to raise money for charity.

Eager to Please

In elementary school, Hillary was studious and worked hard. She earned almost straight As on her report cards. Her academic ability, along with her eagerness to please her teachers, soon earned her the reputation of teacher's pet. Despite her success in school, Hillary could not seem to win her father's full approval. If her report card had only one B, he would ask why she had not received straight As. When she did well, he would question why her teachers had not assigned more challenging work. Hillary later suggested that this was her father's way of always challenging her to do better.

Hugh Rodham was a strict father, although his sons felt his discipline more often than Hillary did. He had grown up during the Great Depression in a time when many families lost everything they had. Because of this, Hugh worried about the possibility of falling into poverty. Hillary was rarely allowed to buy new clothes. The family lived through cold Chicago winter nights without heat, since Hugh turned it off every evening to save money. If he thought his children were being wasteful, he would punish them. For example, he

Standing Up for Herself

When Hillary was four years old, she came home from playing at a neighbor's house and complained that the girl across the street was picking on her. Rather than comfort her daughter, Hillary's mother sent her right back outside and told her to stand up for herself and hit back if necessary. Hillary did—and the bullying stopped.

might throw the cap of the toothpaste outside and make his children go get it, even when there was snow on the ground. Friends of the family also reported that Hugh was often verbally abusive toward his wife.

Political Roots

In the Rodhams' largely conservative neighborhood, Hillary's father was an outspoken Republican, while her mother was a Democrat who tended to hide her views. Both parents' political beliefs had an influence on Hillary. "I grew up between the push and tug of my parents' values, and my own political beliefs reflect both," she wrote in her autobiography *Living History*.[1] The family often had

Women's Roles

Hillary grew up during a time in U.S. history when women's roles were just beginning to change. During the 1940s and 1950s, most women were expected to stay home and raise their families. Yet, Hillary's mother encouraged her to pursue any career that interested her. Dorothy Rodham did not want her daughter's life to be limited as she felt hers had been. Despite the fact that she loved being a mother, Dorothy was sometimes frustrated that she had had so few choices for her future.

At 14, Hillary learned of the limits society sometimes placed on women when she wrote to the National Aeronautics and Space Administration (NASA) to volunteer for the astronaut-training program. The reply she received outraged her: girls were not accepted into the program. She later said that experience was the first time she had encountered such a barrier. She was frustrated by the fact that her usual method of overcoming obstacles—hard work—could not help her in this instance.

lively political discussions around the dinner table. Hillary did not hesitate to express her opinions, even when they differed from those of her parents. While growing up, Hillary generally leaned more strongly toward her father's Republican views.

At the age of 13, Hillary was moved to take political action after John F. Kennedy, a Democrat, won the 1960 presidential election. Influenced by her father's and a teacher's views that the vote had been rigged, Hillary and her friend Betsy Johnson volunteered to help investigate possible vote fraud. Without their parents' permission, the two girls rode a bus to downtown Chicago. They were given voter registration lists to check. Strangers then drove Hillary to a poor neighborhood on Chicago's South Side, where she was left alone to go door-to-door and compare residents' names to her lists. Although Hillary was proud that she had found a few voters registered to an empty lot, her father was furious when he learned she had put herself into such a dangerous situation.

As Hillary grew older, her passion for politics grew. During the 1964

Hillary's Jobs

When Hillary was 13 years old, she earned her first paycheck at a summer job. She was responsible for supervising children at a park near her home. After that, Hillary held a job every summer, and she sometimes worked during the school year as well. Among her jobs were positions at a daycare center and a store.

Hillary in high school

presidential election, she worked as a "Goldwater
Girl." Hillary campaigned for Republican Senator
Barry Goldwater, although he lost the election to
Lyndon Johnson.

HIGH SCHOOL

In high school, Hillary continued to demonstrate the same hard work and dedication to her studies that she had shown in earlier years. She was involved in a wide variety of activities, including the school newspaper, prom committee, and student government. She served as junior class vice president and was part of her school's new cultural values committee. This body was created to encourage understanding between the various groups—such as academics and athletes—in the school.

During her senior year, Hillary ran for student government president. She lost the election. Later, she remembered one of her male opponents telling her she was "really stupid if [she] thought a girl could be elected president."[2]

EXPANDING HORIZONS

While in high school, Hillary was introduced to Reverend Donald Jones, who served as the youth minister at her church. Reverend Jones hosted a youth group that he called the "University of Life." Through it, he encouraged his students to broaden their horizons. He introduced them to important works of literature and art. He also taught them to

Driving

Hillary was eager to get her driver's license when she turned 16, but her father would not allow it. He insisted that if she needed to get somewhere far from home, her friends could drive her. Otherwise, she could ride her bike. Humiliated, Hillary convinced a friend to help her get her license. Her friend was successful, despite the fact that Hillary was not a very good driver.

live a life in which their faith showed through their actions.

With her youth group, Hillary traveled to other churches around Chicago and was introduced to black and Hispanic students. The experience helped shape her views of race: "I learned that, despite the obvious differences in our environments, these kids were more like me than I ever could have imagined."[3]

It was also Reverend Jones who took Hillary to see Martin Luther King Jr. speak in 1961. King's speech made her realize the depth of the civil rights struggle in the United States. It also formed the basis of her lifelong belief that the problems of prejudice and discrimination in the country needed to be addressed. ‿

Hearing Martin Luther King Jr. speak had a profound impact on Hillary's beliefs.

Hillary's high school graduation picture

WOMAN OF WELLESLEY

Growing up, Hillary had never felt that her future would be limited by the fact that she was a girl. Her mother encouraged her to believe that with enough hard work, she could accomplish whatever she wanted. So when it came time for

Hillary to decide what to do after high school, she began to look at colleges.

Initially, she had planned to remain in the Midwest. But during her senior year of high school, two teachers encouraged her to look at Smith College and Wellesley College, women's schools in Massachusetts. Hillary liked Wellesley for several reasons, including that it was an all-women's college. As one graduate of Wellesley said, going to a women's school meant that "you don't have the thing where women don't put their hands up because someone might not take you out because you know the answer and they don't."[1] After being accepted to both colleges, Hillary had to make a decision. She had never visited either school, so she picked Wellesley because the small lake in the campus's photographs reminded her of summers on Lake Winola.

Finding Her Place

When she arrived on campus in the fall of 1965, Hillary did not feel as though she fit in. She had a hard

Wellesley College

Wellesley College was founded in 1870 with the belief that women could handle the same rigorous academic work as men. From its first class of 314 women, Wellesley has grown to a student body of more than 2,000 today. Among notable Wellesley graduates are China's former First Lady Madame Chiang Kai-Shek (1917), former U.S. Secretary of State Madeleine Albright (1959), and television journalist Diane Sawyer (1967).

time with some of her classes in math and geology. She was intimidated by the other students who seemed more sophisticated. This was also her first time away from home alone, and she was homesick.

Only a month after classes began, Hillary called home to tell her parents that she did not think she could make it at Wellesley. Although her father was ready to let Hillary come home, her mother told her not to quit. Hillary listened to her mother's advice and stayed at school.

Soon, Hillary grew accustomed to campus life and began to thrive. She abandoned her desire to become a doctor and turned to courses in political science, which seemed to be a better fit. She began to make friends too. One friend later said that during college Hillary was "fun-loving, full of mischief, spunky, good-natured . . . a wonderfully warm and thoughtful friend."[2]

Hillary gained a reputation as a leader on campus. During her freshman year, she was elected president of the Young Republicans club, despite the fact that she was beginning to have doubts about the Republican Party. In particular, she was concerned about its views on civil rights issues and the Vietnam War. Eventually, her growing discomfort with the

Hillary, center, at Wellesley College

party led her to resign from the position. Hillary also served as a student senate representative her sophomore year. And in February 1968, she was elected college government president.

THE WIDER WORLD

As a campus leader, Hillary played a large role in shaping Wellesley's response to events in the wider world. The 1960s was a tumultuous decade, during which protests rocked many college campuses. Most of the protests were against the Vietnam War or in support of stronger civil rights legislation. On other college campuses, students were turning against authorities, but Hillary encouraged a different approach. She urged Wellesley students to avoid confrontation and to focus instead on constructive conversations and discussions.

From Republican to Democrat

During the summer of 1968, Hillary participated in a nine-week summer internship program in Washington DC. The program was designed to give students an understanding of how government worked by assigning them to a government agency or a congressional office. Hillary had begun to question her former allegiance to the Republican Party and was campaigning for Democrat Eugene McCarthy for the party's presidential nomination. Despite this, Hillary was assigned to work for the House Republican Conference.

When she arrived in Washington DC, Hillary reported for work to Gerald Ford, who was the minority leader in the House of Representatives. Although she was a college student, Hillary was not intimidated by working with Ford and other representatives. On one occasion, she became involved in a heated debate with Congressman Melvin Laird of Wisconsin over his support for the

Vietnam War. Hillary impressed Laird, who later said, "She presented her viewpoints very forcibly, always had ideas, always defended what she had in mind."[3]

As part of her internship, Hillary attended the Republican Convention in Miami, Florida, where the party would choose its candidate for the 1968 presidential race. Hillary helped campaign for Governor Nelson Rockefeller of New York, despite the fact that she knew the moderate governor was likely to lose the nomination to the more conservative

King and the Civil Rights Movement

As a leader of the civil rights movement of the 1950s and 1960s, Martin Luther King Jr. worked to achieve equal rights for blacks. He rose to national prominence in 1955 when he led a bus boycott in the city of Montgomery, Alabama. The boycott was in protest of racial segregation. Blacks were required to sit at the back of a bus and to forfeit their seats to white passengers if a bus became too crowded. After more than one year, segregation on buses was declared unconstitutional.

After the bus boycott, King traveled the country as a leader of the nonviolent movement for equal rights. He led peaceful marches and protests, organized registration drives for black voters, and delivered thousands of impassioned speeches. His most famous speech was "I Have a Dream," in which he spoke of his hope that one day all people of the nation would be truly united.

In 1964, King was awarded the Nobel Peace Prize. Four years later, on April 4, 1968, he was assassinated in Memphis, Tennessee. His assassination had a strong impact on Hillary, who donned a black armband to show her anger and grief.

Richard Nixon. Rockefeller's loss seemed to cement Hillary's opinion that the Republican Party was moving in the wrong direction. She now identified more strongly with the Democratic Party.

A View of Violence

Hillary returned home from the Republican Convention in time for the Democratic Convention, which was being held in Chicago. When violent antiwar riots erupted outside the convention, Hillary and her friend Betsy Johnson decided they needed a firsthand view of the events. They drove to Grant Park, the site of the most violent rioting. What they saw shocked them. Hillary described the scene in *Living History*:

> You could smell the tear gas before you saw the lines of police. In the crowd behind us, someone screamed profanities and threw a rock, which just missed us. Betsy and I scrambled to get away as the police charged the crowd with nightsticks.[4]

That fall, Hillary returned to Wellesley for her senior year, determined to focus the campus's attention more strongly on the antiwar movement. She did not want the violent protests that had rocked Chicago repeated at Wellesley. Instead, she organized teach-ins, which consisted of speeches or lectures directed against the Vietnam War.

THE COMMENCEMENT SPEAKER

As graduation approached, Hillary's classmates at Wellesley began to insist that they have a student commencement speaker. The college had never done this before, and its president was reluctant to allow it. Eventually, after learning that Hillary was the class's choice for speaker, the president relented.

On the day of graduation, May 31, 1969, Hillary was slated to speak after Republican Senator Edward Brooke. In his speech, Brooke largely overlooked the topics that were foremost on the minds of the graduates—the Vietnam War and the civil rights movement—except to speak out against the methods being used by protestors. Disappointed by the senator's speech, Hillary decided to forgo the remarks she had prepared and instead deliver a response to what she had just heard.

Alaska Trip

After graduating from Wellesley, Hillary spent the summer of 1969 in Alaska. In order to pay for her trip, she took on various jobs in the state, including one as a dishwasher in Mount McKinley National Park (now Denali National Park). In the port city of Valdez, she worked at a salmon factory cleaning and packing fish. When she pointed out that some of the salmon had gone bad, she was fired. She never received her last check—when she returned for it, the factory was closed.

During her speech, Hillary defended the right—and responsibility—to protest, saying, "We're not in the positions yet of leadership and power, but we do have [the] indispensable task of criticizing and constructive protest."[5] She talked about how she and her classmates had come to college with high expectations of the world and how, when those expectations were not always met, they had worked for change. She spoke of the need to live with integrity, trust, and respect.

As Hillary closed her speech, the audience rose to its feet for a standing ovation. To her surprise, they were not the only ones who had been impressed by her address. Her parents' house was soon flooded with calls from reporters and talk show hosts. She made an appearance on a Chicago television show and was featured in an article in *Life* magazine. This was her first taste of national recognition.

During her time at Wellesley, Hillary came to be known as a good speaker.

Hillary attended Yale Law School from 1969 to 1973.

STUDYING THE LAW

efore graduating from Wellesley, Hillary had applied to several law schools. When both Harvard and Yale accepted her, she faced a difficult choice. She remained undecided until she met a famous Harvard Law professor who told her,

"We don't need any more women at Harvard."[1] That comment helped her decide to go to Yale.

When Hillary arrived at Yale Law School in 1969, she was part of a class of 235 students. Only 27 were women. Yet, representing more than 10 percent of the class, women were beginning to be taken seriously.

Focus on Families and Children

At Yale, Hillary sharpened her focus on social issues. In the spring of 1970, she served on the board of the new *Yale Review of Law and Social Action*, an alternative to the highly regarded *Yale Law Journal*. The review's purpose was to explore how the law could be used to bring about social change.

In the summer of 1970, Hillary moved to Washington DC to work for the Washington Research Project. The project was directed by Marian Wright Edelman, who soon became a mentor to Hillary. As part of her

Rioting at Yale

The protests that had rocked college campuses during Hillary's years at Wellesley continued during her first years at Yale. In April 1970, eight men belonging to the militant Black Panther group were tried for the murder of one of their members. The trial was held in New Haven, Connecticut, where Yale is located. Angry riots soon broke out across the city. Protestors claimed that the men had been set up by the Federal Bureau of Investigation (FBI).

On April 27, in the midst of these events, someone set fire to the International Law Library at Yale. Hillary and her classmates quickly formed an old-fashioned bucket brigade to put out the flames. After that, they patrolled the campus nightly.

job, Hillary researched the living conditions of migrant farm workers and their families. She found that these families often lacked proper housing and sanitation and that children frequently went without schooling. She reported her findings at Senate hearings headed by Senator Walter Mondale.

Some of Hillary's Yale classmates were at the hearings, too. They were working for law firms that stood on the other side of the issue. Their law firms represented some of the corporations accused of mistreating the migrant workers. Hillary was not afraid to express her disdain for the kind of law her classmates were practicing. "My life is too short to spend it making money for some big anonymous firm," she said.[2]

Hillary later said that her summer working on the Washington Research Project marked a turning point in her life. When she returned to Yale that fall, she focused her studies on family and children's law. She worked with the Yale Child Study Center, part of Yale's School of Medicine, in order to learn more about issues that affected children's development. She also helped the staff at Yale–New Haven Hospital develop legal guidelines for doctors to follow when they suspected a child had been abused.

She partnered with doctors to identify likely cases of child abuse and determine whether to remove abused children from their homes.

Meeting Bill Clinton

Hillary's focus on her studies brought her to the library one night in the spring of 1971. There, she noticed that a man in the hallway kept looking at her. Boldly, she walked up to him and said, "If you're going to keep looking at me, and I'm going to keep looking back, we might as well be introduced. I'm Hillary Rodham."[3] This was Hillary's first encounter with Bill Clinton. After that, the two did not talk again until the end of the semester, when Hillary was on her way to register for the next semester's classes. Bill accompanied her, and when she discovered that he had already registered, he admitted that he had just wanted to be with her. The two soon became a couple.

Children's Advocacy

During her time at Yale, Hillary worked with the New Haven Legal Services office, which provided legal aid to poor local residents. As part of her work, Hillary represented a woman who wanted to adopt her two-year-old foster child. Hillary helped the woman sue Connecticut's social services department, which prohibited foster parents from adopting their foster children. Although they lost the case, it led Hillary to an important realization: she wanted to use the law to speak for children who could not speak for themselves.

Hillary and Bill on the Yale campus

That summer, Hillary and Bill traveled together to California, where Hillary clerked at the small law office of Treuhaft, Walker, and Burnstein, a radical practice known for its civil liberties work. Although

Bill had planned to spend the summer campaigning for Democratic presidential candidate George McGovern, he had given up his plans to be with Hillary. When they returned for the fall 1971 semester at Yale, the two rented a house together.

Moving On

Two years later, in 1973, both Bill and Hillary graduated from Yale Law School. Afterward, they traveled to England together. There, Bill asked Hillary to marry him. She said no, later explaining that she was not ready.

When they returned from their trip abroad, Bill and Hillary went their own ways. Bill returned to his home state of Arkansas to teach at the University of Arkansas School of Law. Hillary moved to Cambridge, Massachusetts, to work at the new Children's Defense Fund, headed by her mentor Marian Wright

Published Article

In 1974, Hillary's first scholarly article, "Children Under the Law," was published in the prestigious *Harvard Educational Review*. In the article, Hillary discussed rights of young people under 18, which were then considered minors under the law. She said that children do not suddenly become competent adults on the day they turn 18, but mature slowly during their childhood and teen years. She held that the law should consider each child's level of competence on a case-by-case basis.

Edelman. As part of her job, Hillary was responsible for investigating and reporting on low school enrollment rates. Her job also took her to South Carolina, where she spent time talking with juvenile offenders who were serving time in adult prisons.

Bill Clinton's Background

Bill Clinton, who was named William Jefferson Blythe at birth, was born on August 19, 1946, in Hope, Arkansas. His father, William Blythe, died in a car accident three months before Bill's birth. Bill and his mother, Virginia, lived with Virginia's parents, who helped raise the boy. Virginia left Arkansas for a time to study nursing in New Orleans, while Bill remained with his grandparents. When Bill was four years old, his mother returned to Arkansas and married Roger Clinton. Bill's stepfather often drank too much and was abusive, but as a teenager, Bill took Roger's last name.

Bill was a bright student who excelled at playing the saxophone. For a time, he considered pursuing a music career. As a high school senior, though, he had the opportunity to meet President John F. Kennedy at the White House. It was a defining moment for Bill. After that, he was determined to dedicate his life to public service. Before entering Yale, Bill attended Georgetown University, graduating in 1968 with a degree in international affairs. He then spent a year as a Rhodes Scholar studying government at Oxford University in England.

Investigating Impeachment

In January 1974, Hillary was offered a position on the team investigating the potential impeachment of President Richard Nixon. The president was being investigated for his involvement in the Watergate scandal, in which the Democratic Party's headquarters had been robbed and wiretapped. Although Hillary found her work with the Children's Defense Fund exciting and rewarding, she accepted this new venture. "I couldn't imagine a more important mission at this juncture in American history," she said.[4]

Leaving her job in Massachusetts, 26-year-old Hillary moved to Washington DC and joined a team of 44 lawyers working on the impeachment inquiry. Most, like Hillary, were young, but some were renowned lawyers. Rising just after the sun came up, Hillary and her colleagues put in 12- to 18-hour days. Hillary served as part of a team that analyzed the White House decision-making process. She also spent time researching impeachment procedures and summarizing the legal grounds for impeachment.

On July 19, 1974, the head of the investigation, John Doar, presented articles of impeachment to the

Watergate

In June 1972, five men were arrested for burglarizing the Democratic Party's national headquarters, located at the Watergate office complex in Washington DC. The men had been hired by the Republican Party's Committee to Re-elect the President. The impeachment investigation was intended to discover President Nixon's level of involvement in the affair. The House Judiciary Committee approved articles of impeachment after learning that Nixon had tried to conceal the burglary, paid off witnesses, and misused Internal Revenue Service (IRS) records. The Watergate scandal led Nixon to become the first U.S. president to resign from office.

Impeachment

Impeachment is the process by which charges are brought against a government official. In the case of a federal official, the charges are brought by the U.S. House of Representatives. According to the U.S. Constitution, an official can be impeached for treason, bribery, or high crimes and misdemeanors, although it does not specify the crimes that fall within this category. After being impeached, an official is tried by the Senate.

House Judiciary Committee, which passed three of them. Less than a month later, on August 9, Nixon resigned from the presidency. With his resignation, "one of the most intense and significant experiences" of Hillary's life came to an end.[5]

*In 1974, Hillary worked on a team that investigated the potential
impeachment of President Richard Nixon.*

Hillary's mother, Hillary, and Bill on the Clintons' wedding day

MOVING SOUTH

With the job on the impeachment inquiry complete, Hillary again had a decision to make about her future. This time, she decided to move to Arkansas to be with Bill. Although her friends were surprised that she would move so far from the nation's center of power, Hillary was determined to give her relationship with Bill a chance—even if it meant moving to Arkansas. "It was never in the game plan to grow up and fall in love with someone from Arkansas," she said.[1]

Hillary accepted a job teaching at the University of Arkansas School of Law in Fayetteville, the same school where Bill taught. In addition to teaching courses on criminal law and trial advocacy, Hillary was assigned to direct the school's legal aid clinic and prison project. She supervised students as they provided legal services to poor residents and prisoners.

When Hillary moved to Arkansas, Bill was in the middle of a bid for a seat in the U.S. Congress. If Bill won the race, he and Hillary would relocate to Washington DC. Hillary helped with the campaign, as did her father and her brother Tony. Despite their efforts, Bill lost a close race, winning 48 percent of the vote to his opponent's 52 percent. Hillary and Bill remained in Arkansas.

The Clintons' Teaching

Although Bill and Hillary taught at the same law school, they had very different teaching styles. Hillary's classes tended to be structured and demanding, while Bill's were laid-back and conversational. He was an easy grader, while she gave difficult exams. Students who took classes with both Bill and Hillary concluded that they learned more from Hillary's classes but that Bill's were more interesting.

SAYING "YES"

Despite the fact that she had moved to Arkansas, Hillary still was not sure if she could make the state her permanent home. In the fall of 1975, she took a trip to the East Coast and Chicago, following up on job leads and trying to decide what to do next.

By the end of her trip, Hillary had decided to remain in Arkansas with Bill, and when she returned there, she found that he had a surprise for her. Before her trip, Hillary had pointed out a brick house that was for sale. Bill told her that he had bought it, adding, "So now you'd better marry me because I can't live in it by myself."[2] This time, Hillary said yes. The wedding was held on October 11, 1975, in the living room of Bill and Hillary's new house.

POLITICS AND PRIVATE PRACTICE

The next year, Bill was elected attorney general of Arkansas, which meant that the couple had to move to Little Rock. Although few women in Little Rock pursued careers, Hillary was determined to continue in the law profession, especially since Bill's salary as attorney general would be fairly small. Seeking to avoid any job that might present a conflict of interest with her husband's position, Hillary decided to join a private firm. She was offered a position with the Rose Law Firm, one of the most respected law offices in the state. She became the firm's first female lawyer.

Hillary was driven and intense at the Rose Law Firm. As the company's only female lawyer, she faced scrutiny from some female secretaries. They gossiped about her unfeminine characteristics, including her clothes, hairstyle, and ambition. In her first years at the firm, Hillary found she did not do her best work inside a courtroom. Thereafter, she appeared only occasionally in front of a judge and jury.

As Hillary focused on her work with the Rose Law Firm, Bill decided to run for governor of Arkansas. Although Hillary did little work on the campaign, she won the admiration of some, who thought that if Bill were elected, he and his wife could both make a difference for the state. Others, though, were critical of Hillary because she was

A Failed Exam

In order to obtain a license to practice law in a particular state, a lawyer must pass a test called the bar exam. After graduating from Yale in 1973, Hillary had taken two bar exams, one in Washington DC and one in Arkansas. She passed the exam in Arkansas but failed the Washington DC exam. Hillary kept her failure a secret for 30 years, only revealing it in her autobiography, *Living History*. Although she could have taken the exam again, it was no longer necessary. Hillary made the choice to live in Arkansas instead of Washington DC.

an independent, career-focused wife. They were especially upset that Hillary had chosen to keep her own last name, Rodham, rather than take her husband's last name.

Despite the criticism leveled at Hillary, Bill won the 1978 gubernatorial election. He and Hillary moved into the redbrick governor's mansion in downtown Little Rock. That same year, President Jimmy Carter appointed Hillary to serve on the board of the nation's Legal Services Corporation. This corporation was responsible for overseeing the allocation of funds

What's in a Name?

Hillary's decision to keep her last name when she married Bill was an issue in Arkansas. When Bill told his mother, Virginia, that Hillary would not be taking the name Clinton, she broke down in tears. The guests at the couple's wedding were also shocked by the news. The wedding announcement in the *Arkansas Democrat-Gazette* stressed that Hillary would remain Hillary Rodham.

Hillary's decision not to take her husband's name dated back to her childhood. She had always felt that her name was part of her identity. Hillary was genuinely surprised by people's reaction to her decision:

I kept my maiden name when I married because it was important to me that I be judged on my merits and that Bill be judged on his merits . . . but I was not at all prepared about the concern people expressed about this decision, which we had made personally.[3]

Hillary later said that Bill was the only person who had not pressured her to change her name. Ultimately, Hillary said that she came to the conclusion that she would rather see Bill be governor again than keep her last name.

In 1979, Hillary and Bill attended a White House dinner for governors.

to legal services offices within each state. The next year, Hillary was made a partner at the Rose Law Firm, a high position in a firm usually held by only a few lawyers.

In addition to her work responsibilities, Hillary was actively involved in Bill's governorship. Rather than focusing solely on fulfilling the traditional social role of a political wife, Hillary worked with Bill

An Outspoken Wife

During Bill's 1982 run for governor, Hillary was a visible part of the campaign. At one point, she attended an event at which her husband's opponent, Frank White, was speaking. When he started talking about Bill's record, she accused him of lying. White was shocked—this was an unexpected role for a political wife. Her actions earned Hillary the praise of the *Arkansas Democrat-Gazette*, which said she was "almost certainly the best speaker among politicians' wives."[6]

in shaping policy. She chaired his Rural Health Advisory Committee, which worked to improve rural health care in the state.

Changes

In 1979, Hillary became pregnant. She and Bill had long wanted to have children, and both were thrilled with the news. On February 27, 1980, Bill returned from a meeting in Washington DC in time to take his wife to the hospital to give birth to their daughter, Chelsea Victoria Clinton. Hillary later said that Chelsea's birth was "the most miraculous and awe-inspiriting event" in her life.[4] She wrote,

> *Chelsea's birth transformed our lives, bringing us the greatest gift of joy—and humility—any parent could hope for. Like every child, Chelsea was her own person from the beginning. . . . I prayed that I would be a good enough mother for her.*[5]

The year Chelsea was born, Bill ran for reelection as Arkansas's governor and lost. Although he was devastated by the defeat, Hillary helped convince

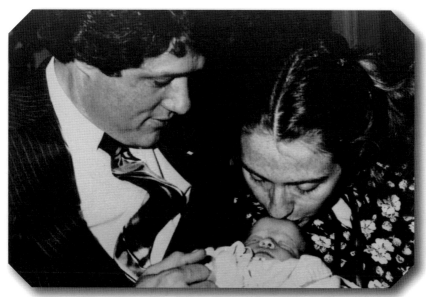

Hillary and Bill with their daughter, Chelsea, in 1980

him to run again in 1982. This time, Hillary was
closely involved with the campaign. To keep her last
name from becoming an issue that might hurt Bill
in the election, she decided to become known as
Hillary Rodham Clinton. Bill won the election, and
the family moved back into the governor's mansion.
Bill was reelected three more times, and the family
remained in Little Rock until early 1993.

Hillary continued to be involved in policy making
at the state level. Bill appointed her to chair his
newly formed Education Standards Committee,

saying, "This guarantees that I will have a person who is closer to me than anyone else overseeing a project that is more important to me than anything else."[7]

"[Bill and Hillary] don't do anything that isn't strongly. Whether it's agree or disagree, it's strongly. They are two of the most passionate people I ever met. They love passionately, they argue passionately, they parent passionately, they read passionately, they play passionately."[8]

—*Betsey Wright, chief of staff for Bill Clinton, 1982–1989*

Hillary took a leave of absence from her job at the Rose Law Firm in order to devote her time to education reform. At the time, Arkansas had one of the worst education systems in the country. Many of its schools offered no foreign language, music, physics, or advanced math classes. Its students scored low on achievement tests, and reports told of teachers who could barely read.

In order to address these issues, Hillary's committee suggested raising taxes to improve schools, adding more standardized tests, standardizing school curriculums, and implementing teacher testing. Her reform efforts seemed to make a difference in the state. The number of students going on to college increased, class sizes were reduced, and foreign language, advanced math, and science courses became standard.

Bill and Hillary celebrating Bill's election as Arkansas governor in 1982

Bill and Hillary during the 1992 presidential campaign

REDEFINING
THE FIRST LADY

*A*ccording to friends, Hillary had long
thought that Bill Clinton would one day
be president. As the 1992 election year approached,
she and Bill decided that the time was right for him
to run for the office. On October 3, 1991, Bill

announced his candidacy. Hillary took a leave of absence from her job at the Rose Law Firm in order to play an active role on the campaign trail. She helped her husband develop strategy and spoke on his behalf at events around the country.

Hillary soon learned that she had to be careful not to appear too powerful, however. At one campaign stop, Bill joked that if voters put him in office, they would get Hillary for free. Although he wanted to show that Hillary's experience would be an asset in the White House, some took his statement to mean that Hillary sought a copresidency. By the end of the campaign, Hillary had taken on a quieter role, applauding her husband's speeches rather than making so many of her own.

Becoming the First Lady

On November 3, 1992, Bill Clinton was elected the nation's forty-second president. He was sworn in on January 20, 1993. Hillary and Chelsea held the Bible for his

On Traditional Values

On the campaign trail during the 1992 presidential race, Hillary was questioned about whether her law career had conflicted with Bill's work as governor. In reply, she said, "I suppose I could have stayed home and baked cookies and had teas, but what I decided to do was fulfill my profession."[1] Immediately, she tried to clarify that women should be free to choose whether to pursue a career or to stay home, but it was too late. Detractors saw her "cookies and teas" comment as proof that she opposed traditional values.

inauguration. Afterward, the family rode down Pennsylvania Avenue toward the White House. They stepped out of their limousine to walk the last couple blocks. Supporters enthusiastically cheered from the roadsides. After watching the three-hour inaugural parade, the Clinton family finally headed into their new home around 6:00 p.m. Hillary later described the moment:

> *It was during my walk up the path toward the White House and up the stairs of the North Portico and into the Grand Foyer that the reality hit me: I was actually the First Lady, married to the President of the United States.*[2]

DEFINING HER ROLE

Hillary was the First Lady, and she was ready to define that role for herself. As she pointed out, "There is no training manual for first ladies."[3] Traditionally, the First Lady is expected to oversee ceremonial and social events at the White House. Hillary accepted this role, but at the same time, she expected to be a vital part of her husband's administration.

Although the wives of former presidents had worked from an office in the East Wing of the White

House, Hillary set up her office in the West Wing. She became one of Bill's most trusted advisors and often sat in on senior staff meetings. She was involved in everything from polishing the president's speeches to helping direct domestic policy. One White House staff member summarized Hillary's role:

> *A speech that needs a rewrite, get Hillary. A speech that needs to be given, get Hillary. The President has a problem he wants to chew over, get Hillary. The point is you never go wrong getting Hillary.*[4]

Hillary's Father Dies

Just two months after Bill took office, on March 19, 1993, Hillary's father had a stroke. Hillary left Washington DC to be with him in Little Rock, Arkansas, where she remained for two weeks. The experience had a powerful impact on her, and it colored an emotional speech she delivered in Austin, Texas, on April 6. In her speech, she wondered aloud about the beginning and end of life and talked about the importance of family values. Her father died the next day.

HEALTH CARE

Only four days after Bill had officially taken office, he announced that he had appointed Hillary chair of his Task Force on National Health Care Reform, which would develop a universal health care policy to be taken to Congress. Universal health care is a policy that provides health insurance for all residents of a government region, either by federal or private funding or a combination of both. In his

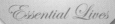

autobiography *My Life*, Bill explained his decision:

> *Heading up the effort to reform health care was an unprecedented thing for a First Lady to do. . . . I decided Hillary should lead the health-care effort because she cared and knew a lot about the issue, she had time to do the job right, and I thought she would be an honest broker among all the competing interests.*[5]

With the goal of providing a reform proposal to Congress within 100 days, Hillary set to work. It soon became apparent, however, that it would take more than 100 days to gather all the needed information from the more than 500 experts working to develop the policy. The deadline came and went, but Hillary kept working. Throughout this time, Hillary endured scathing criticism from Republicans who believed her reform policy would mean government-run health care. In September 1993, she appeared before several House and Senate committees to speak about health care reform. Although she wowed many senators and representatives who heard her speak, the complicated bill she presented to them was defeated in 1994. Health care reform had failed.

*Hillary appeared on several magazine covers
during her first weeks as First Lady.*

Taking a Backseat

Her failure to pass a health care reform bill led
Hillary to rethink her position in her husband's
administration. She decided to take more of a
backseat role. She worked behind the scenes to assist
with welfare reform efforts and to prevent cuts to
education and health care programs.

Despite her new background role, Hillary
began to serve as a U.S. representative overseas.
In March 1995, Hillary flew to Asia at the request
of the U.S. State Department, which wanted to
demonstrate U.S. commitment to that part of the

world. Although Bill remained in Washington DC, 15-year-old Chelsea accompanied her mother on the trip. In addition to meeting with the leaders of several countries, including Pakistan and India, Hillary and Chelsea met with villagers, especially women and girls. The mother and daughter learned about other women's daily lives and challenges.

Speaking Up for Women's Rights

Only six months after her trip to Asia, Hillary returned to the continent. This time she visited China to address the United Nations Fourth World Conference on Women. In a country known for its human rights violations, Hillary was to give a speech about human rights abuses against women. She needed to be careful not to offend her host nation while giving a strong voice to the cause of human rights.

Health Care Reform Protests

As part of her effort to generate support for her health care reform bill, Hillary took part in a national bus tour called the Health Security Express during the summer of 1994. Rather than cheering supporters, however, Hillary found angry mobs at her first stops on the tour. Protestors objected to the reform bill, which they said would launch socialized, or government-run, health care. As she spoke in Seattle, Washington, protestors yelled so loudly that much of her speech could not be heard. When she left, a huge, angry mob surrounded her limousine. Two guns and a knife were found among the protestors.

Standing before audience members from around the world, Hillary began to speak of women's contributions to society. She talked about the need for women to be healthy and educated in order for their families to flourish. Then she listed human rights violations to which women were too often subjected. These included physical abuse, rape, and forced prostitution. She also spoke of the denial of education and the right to vote. She said, "If there is one message that echoes forth from this

Eleanor and Hillary

Perhaps the most influential of all First Ladies before Hillary was Eleanor Roosevelt, wife of President Franklin Roosevelt, who served from 1932 to 1945. She held her own press conferences, had a radio show, and wrote a newspaper column. She was a vocal supporter of civil rights and spoke on behalf of working women and migrant workers. Hillary greatly admires Eleanor Roosevelt and has said that she sometimes had imaginary conversations with the former First Lady, trying to figure out what Eleanor would do in a given situation.

Comparisons have been drawn between Hillary and Eleanor. Both women had successful careers tied to their presidential husbands as well as on their own. Both women experienced harsh criticism for their political actions. However, criticism of Hillary may have stemmed from another cause. Historian Doris Kearns Goodwin stated,

Men didn't worry that their wives were going to wake up in the morning and want to be Eleanor Roosevelt. . . . But Hillary is part of a whole movement of women becoming important in all sectors of life. . . . And I think to the extent that she got to be the symbol of that forward-looking, aggressive woman . . . people did project onto her things that she hadn't even deserved.[6]

In 1995, Hillary addressed attendees of the United Nations Fourth World Conference on Women in China.

conference, let it be that human rights are women's rights and women's rights are human rights once and for all."[7]

As Hillary concluded her speech with a call for all those in attendance to work for improved women's rights in their own countries, audience members jumped to their feet to give her a standing ovation. When she left the hall, people surrounded her, reaching out to touch her hand and thank her. Although the displeased Chinese government kept the speech off state television and radio, Hillary's remarks made the front pages of newspapers around the world. An editorial in the *New York Times* said the speech "may have been her finest moment in public life."[8]

TROUBLE IN THE WHITE HOUSE

Despite her success in China, Hillary was not without trouble at home. In January 1996, she was called to testify before a grand jury. For more than two years, federal investigators had been looking into Hillary's involvement in a real estate transaction known as Whitewater. Whitewater referred to a property in Arkansas that the Clintons had purchased with friends Jim and Susan McDougal. They had planned to develop the property and sell lots for vacation homes. However, they lost money on the deal when the lots did not sell.

The investigation centered on charges that Jim McDougal had illegally financed Bill's 1986 gubernatorial campaign. McDougal had allegedly done so through his savings and loan company, a type of savings institution that helps others build

Chelsea in the White House

Chelsea was nearly 13 when the Clintons moved into the White House. Both Bill and Hillary were determined to give her a normal life. Hillary kept her own afternoons free so that she would be around when Chelsea came home from school. Both she and Bill tried to be home for dinner most nights. Like other kids her age, Chelsea played soccer and took ballet lessons. And she often invited friends to the White House to hang out in her two rooms on the second floor.

and purchase homes. As part of the investigation, Hillary had been requested to turn over billing records that documented the work she had done for McDougal's company while a lawyer at the Rose Law Firm. For two years, Hillary said that the records were lost. But in early January 1996, she reported that they had been found. Now the grand jury wanted to know where the billing records had been for the past two years. They were trying to figure out if she or anyone else had been obstructing justice by keeping them hidden. Hillary testified for four hours, insisting that she was baffled by the records' disappearance and reappearance. It was later determined that she had done nothing illegal in regard to Whitewater.

When she had finished testifying, Hillary gratefully returned to the White House. She had no way of knowing that the Whitewater investigation would create even bigger problems during her husband's second term.

Hillary spoke with reporters before testifying in front of a grand jury in regard to Whitewater.

Hillary spoke at the 1996 Democratic National Convention on August 27.

PERSONAL AND PUBLIC TRIALS

s Bill hit the presidential campaign trail in 1996, Hillary remained relatively uninvolved in his race for reelection. At the end of August, though, she gave a speech at the Democratic National Convention in support of her husband's candidacy. Although other First Ladies had addressed national political conventions—beginning with Eleanor Roosevelt in 1940—Hillary was the first whose speech was televised. On the night of August 27, Hillary walked into the United Center in Chicago to the applause of 20,000 people. In her speech, Hillary focused largely on the areas that had always concerned her most: children and families. She asked the audience to think about what the world would be like in 32 years, when Chelsea was her age. She said that although no one could know what the future would bring,

> One thing we know for sure is that change is certain. Progress is not. Progress depends on the choices we make today for tomorrow and on whether we meet our challenges and protect our values.[1]

In November, Bill won his bid for reelection. As she celebrated her husband's second inauguration as president, Hillary felt like she was more prepared for the challenge of being First Lady than she had been in 1993. "I felt I was entering this new chapter of my life like steel tempered in fire: a bit harder at the edges but more durable, more flexible," she wrote in *Living History*.[2]

WORKING FOR FAMILIES

During Bill's second term, Hillary directed her efforts toward issues affecting women, children, and families. Her successful women's rights speech in China had made Hillary an international figure. She now received requests to speak in countries around the world. Traveling alone or with the president, Hillary gave speeches and attended meetings in countries from Australia and Thailand to South Africa and Zimbabwe.

At the same time, Hillary also

It Takes a Village

Hillary's dedication to issues concerning women, children, and families led her to write the book *It Takes a Village: And Other Lessons Children Teach Us.* Published in 1996, the book's title comes from an African proverb, which holds that it takes a village to raise a child. In the book, Hillary discussed the problems that face families and suggested that parents need the support of the whole "village"—family, churches, schools, and government—to help them raise healthy, successful children.

Some of Hillary's opponents charged that she was advocating government control of family decisions. She addressed their accusations in her speech at the 1996 Democratic National Convention:

For Bill and me, there has been no experience more challenging, more rewarding, and more humbling than raising our daughter. And we have learned that to raise a happy, healthy, and hopeful child, it takes a family. It takes teachers. It takes clergy. It takes business people. It takes community leaders. It takes those who protect our health and safety. It takes all of us. Yes, it takes a village. And it takes a president. . . . It takes Bill Clinton.[3]

maintained an interest in domestic health and family issues. In 1997, she helped establish the Children's Health Insurance Program, which provided insurance to children whose parents could not afford it. She also helped pass the Adoption and Safe Families Act of 1997 to address the issue of foster care adoptions.

In the fall of 1997, Hillary was also getting ready for changes within her own family. Although Hillary had hoped that Chelsea would choose to attend Wellesley or another college nearby, her daughter had selected Stanford University in California. In September, Bill and Hillary brought Chelsea to the college and left her in the protection of Secret Service agents.

THE MONICA LEWINSKY SCANDAL

A little more than one year later, Hillary and Bill's relationship faced its biggest challenge ever.

White House Pets

Like many other presidential families, the Clintons had pets in the White House. They brought their cat, Socks, when they moved into the White House in 1993. After Chelsea left for college in 1997, Hillary gave Bill a chocolate lab puppy named Buddy to keep him company. Although the animals did not get along, both became famous and even inspired a number of fan Web sites.

Hillary spent much of her time as First Lady working for children's rights.

On January 21, 1998, newspapers reported that Bill had been involved in an affair with former White House intern Monica Lewinsky. The reports alleged that he had asked her to lie about the affair. They also alleged that he had lied about it under oath when he testified in a sexual harassment case brought against him by Paula Jones. Although Bill insisted that Lewinsky was lying, Attorney General Janet Reno allowed Kenneth Starr, the independent counsel who investigated Whitewater, to widen his search to include this new accusation.

When Bill told Hillary that he had done nothing wrong, she believed him. She stood up for him to the press, saying that the story was part of a conspiracy by conservatives to negatively impact her husband. For the next seven months, the investigation into the Lewinsky scandal continued. During this time, the Clintons traveled to Africa together and addressed human rights issues in China.

Then, on August 15, 1998, Bill confessed to Hillary that he had been involved in a brief, inappropriate relationship with Lewinsky. Hillary was shocked, hurt, and furious. She was unsure whether her relationship with Bill could continue.

Stevie Wonder

After Bill's confession of his involvement with Monica Lewinsky, Hillary received support and encouragement from a number of people. In September 1998, musician Stevie Wonder asked Hillary if he could play a song he had written for her. The song was about forgiveness, and as Wonder played, Hillary moved her chair closer and closer to the piano. Afterward, the two talked about what it meant to forgive. Hillary later said that this was one of the greatest acts of kindness she received during the Lewinsky scandal.

Deciding to Forgive

Soon after Bill's confession, Hillary, Bill, and Chelsea took a previously scheduled vacation to Martha's Vineyard, Massachusetts. At first, Hillary barely spoke to her husband, and they were rarely in the same room. By the end of the ten-day trip, however, they were beginning to talk again. She realized that she still loved Bill. Although she was angered by what he had done, she felt that it was an issue to be dealt with between her and her husband, not between her husband and the nation. She later wrote,

> I hadn't decided whether to fight for my husband and my marriage, but I was resolved to fight for my President. . . . I believe what my husband did was morally wrong. So was lying to me and misleading the American people about it. I also knew his failing was not a betrayal of his country. [4]

By September, Hillary decided that she did want to fight for her husband and her marriage. Hillary's struggle seemed to make her more sympathetic to the American people. Her approval rating skyrocketed to an all-time high of 70 percent. Some people, however, condemned her for remaining with Bill after his affair.

FIGHTING IMPEACHMENT

In September 1998, Starr concluded his investigation into Bill's actions and presented a recommendation for impeachment to the House Judiciary Committee. Hillary, who thought the impeachment process was being misused, threw herself into campaigning for the Democrats in Congress who were up for reelection that year. She hoped that if the Democrats did well, the Republicans might give up their call for impeachment. Hillary traveled from state to state, rallying support behind the Democratic contenders. Even after developing a blood clot behind her knee, she continued her hectic schedule, although a nurse now accompanied her.

Hillary's efforts helped the Democrats win a few new seats in the House, but this was not enough to prevent the impeachment of her

World Traveler

In the course of her eight years as First Lady, Hillary visited many countries. During her travels, she met with many female leaders from around the world, including Queen Elizabeth II of England, Prime Minister Gro Brundtland of Norway, and Violeta Chamorro, the first female president of Nicaragua.

Presidential Impeachment Trials

The only president other than Bill Clinton who was tried by the Senate was Andrew Johnson. Like Bill, Johnson was ultimately acquitted.

husband. In December, the House voted to impeach Bill for perjury and obstruction of justice. He faced a five-week trial in the U.S. Senate. When it ended in February, he was acquitted of both charges. ⌐

Hillary preparing to speak after the vote to impeach her husband

On February 6, 2000, Hillary announced her candidacy for the U.S. Senate.

SENATOR CLINTON

While Bill was in the midst of his trial in the Senate, Hillary was being encouraged by top Democrats to consider making a bid for a seat in that body in the 2000 election. In November 1998, Senator Daniel Patrick Moynihan

of New York announced that he had decided not
to run for reelection. Many Democrats wanted
Hillary to run for his seat. At first, Hillary declined,
saying that she was preoccupied with other matters
(primarily Bill's trial) and that a Democrat from
New York would be better positioned to win. She
also was not sure that she was up for the rigors of
another political campaign. As Democrats continued
to press her, however, Hillary gave the matter more
thought.

On February 12, 1999, the same day that the
Senate voted to acquit her husband, Hillary met
with Harold Ickes. A former deputy chief of staff
to Bill and an authority on New York politics, Ickes
discussed her chances of winning a Senate seat. He
told Hillary that she would face many challenges in
the race. She was not from New York, had never
lived there, and had no experience of her own in
running for public office. Despite Ickes's concerns,
however, Hillary announced on February 16, 1999,
that she was considering a run and would make her
decision in the coming months.

Hillary had been offered a number of other jobs,
including a foundation director, a talk show host,
and a college president. Ultimately, though, she

decided that if she wanted to continue to work on the issues that were most important to her, she would have to do so from the inside—from the Senate—where the laws affecting those issues were passed.

RUNNING A CAMPAIGN

In January 2000, Hillary moved into a new home in Chappaqua, New York, in order to become an official resident of the state and eligible to run for senator. The next month, she formally announced that she would run. She started spending time on the campaign trail, attempting to convince New Yorkers to vote for someone who had just moved to their state.

As part of her campaign, Hillary held a "listening tour." She traveled to all 62 counties in New York to meet with small groups of voters and listen to their concerns. Rather than focusing on her own views, she asked voters about theirs. She wanted to demonstrate that although she was

Daring to Compete

Hillary was still undecided about running for a Senate seat when she attended an event to promote an HBO documentary about women in sports called *Dare to Compete: The Struggle of Women in Sports.* The event was held at the Lab School in Manhattan. There, the school's basketball captain, Sofia Totti, told Hillary that she, too, should dare to compete. After that, Hillary realized that this was her chance to do what she had been telling women around the world to do—get involved in politics to make a difference.

Hillary campaigning in Ithaca, New York, in 2000

not a New Yorker, she cared about what New Yorkers thought. The days were long, but Hillary enjoyed the campaign and said that being on the trail energized her. Chelsea, who was now a senior at Stanford, joined her mother as often as she could.

During the early stages of the campaign, Hillary's opponent was Republican Rudolph Giuliani, the mayor of New York City. In May 2000, just as she began to overtake him in the polls, Giuliani withdrew from the race. He had been diagnosed with prostate cancer and was involved in a widely publicized marital scandal. Hillary's new opponent was Congressman Rick Lazio. Although the change in opponents was unexpected, Hillary maintained her momentum. On election day, she won by a wide margin.

THE SENATOR

In January 2001, Hillary began her first term as a U.S. senator. She seemed to flourish in her new role. Rather than bursting onto the scene with her own demands and agenda, Hillary spoke carefully and listened attentively to her colleagues, continuing the leadership style she had developed during her listening tour. She did not shy away from the senators who had been involved in the effort to remove her husband from office. Instead, she often worked with them to pass legislation. Hillary's colleagues came to see her as a hardworking senator who did not seek attention—although she often got it simply because of who she was.

LEADING AFTER 9/11

Less than a year after beginning her Senate career, on the morning of September 11, 2001, Hillary was on her way to a meeting when she learned that two planes had crashed into the twin towers of the World Trade Center in New York City. Her first thought was for Chelsea, who was living in Manhattan at the time. Although she could not immediately reach her daughter's phone, Chelsea later called to let her mother know she was safe.

After the attacks, all of Hillary's efforts were directed toward ensuring that the people of New York City had the resources they needed to recover. She later wrote, "That September morning changed me and what I had to do as a Senator, a New Yorker, and an American."[1] On September 12, Hillary flew to New York City, where she examined the wreckage at Ground Zero and talked with rescue officials and volunteers. Later that week, she and fellow New York Senator Charles Schumer traveled to the White House to meet with President George W. Bush. They requested $20 billion for New York City's recovery. The president agreed. As it became clear that the contaminated air at Ground Zero was causing health problems for rescue workers, Hillary convinced Congress to fund further research into the

Senate Committees

During her first years in the Senate, Hillary served on the Health, Education, Labor & Pensions Committee; the Environment and Public Works Committee; and the Budget Committee. She was later appointed to the Armed Services Committee and served on the Special Committee on Aging.

site's air quality. She also sought increased health care benefits for those who were affected.

As she worked to help New Yorkers rebuild, Hillary did not forget that her country had been attacked. She promised to stand behind the president as he sought to bring the terrorists responsible for the attacks to justice. She was in favor of the president's decision to invade Afghanistan, where the leadership of al-Qaeda, the organization deemed responsible for the attacks, was based. She also supported the Patriot Act. This act gave law enforcement officials expanded surveillance and wiretapping capabilities, which they argued were necessary to catch future terrorists.

In October 2002, Hillary and her fellow senators were asked to vote on a resolution to authorize a war against Iraq as part of the nation's new "war on terror." On October 10, Hillary stood in front of the Senate to speak about the resolution. She said that although it did not appear that Iraq's leader, Saddam Hussein, was involved

Remembering Those Lost

On the evening of September 11, 2001, Hillary and more than 100 other members of Congress stood on the steps of the Capitol building to pay their respects to those who had been lost in that day's attacks. After listening to brief remarks by House Speaker Dennis Hastert and Senate Majority Leader Tom Daschle, they observed a moment of silence. Then, someone began to sing "God Bless America." Soon, everyone had joined in. Hillary, too, sang, with tears in her eyes.

in the 9/11 attacks, he was a tyrant known to have harbored terrorists and to have developed weapons of mass destruction. Although she expressed concern about the result of an attack on Iraq and urged the president to first seek the involvement of the United Nations, she said that she had ultimately decided to support the resolution:

> *This is a difficult vote. This is probably the hardest decision I have ever had to make. Any vote that may lead to war should be hard, but I cast it with conviction.* [2]

WORKING FOR THE PEOPLE

September 11 and its aftermath were not the only important aspects

Hillary's Faith

After becoming a senator, Hillary joined one of the Senate's many prayer groups. This was a natural step, since she had been involved with church and prayer groups since her childhood. Hillary had been baptized at the Court Street Methodist Church in Scranton, Pennsylvania, and confirmed at the First United Methodist Church of Park Ridge, Illinois. She had been an active youth group member during her childhood and teenage years. As an adult, Hillary had occasionally taught Bible classes. She also served as a lay, or nonclergy, preacher. During her years in the White House, she was part of a prayer group that included many politicians' wives, both Democrats and Republicans. She credited this group with helping her get through her most difficult times in Washington DC.

Many people close to Hillary have said that her faith is an essential part of who she is. According to one of her aides, "Hillary's faith is the link. . . . It explains the missionary zeal with which she attacks her issues."[3] Hillary once said that she believed it was her duty as a Christian to help the suffering.

of Hillary's work in the Senate. She also continued to work for the causes that had interested her throughout her public life, including health and family issues. She introduced legislation to lower the cost of prescription medications, to increase supplies of influenza vaccine, and to provide better health coverage for low-income HIV patients. She also cosponsored a bill to offer incentives to individuals adopting older and special needs children from the foster care system.

To help communities wrestling with job loss, Hillary worked to pass the Renewal Communities program. She also sought to bring high-speed Internet service to rural communities. In 2006, Hillary turned her attention to energy issues. She tried, but failed, to introduce legislation that would have used taxes on oil companies to fund research into alternative energy sources, such as wind and solar power. Later that year, she was reelected to the Senate with more than two-thirds of the vote. By then, she had begun to set her sights on an even higher office.

On September 12, 2001, Hillary visited the site of the fallen World Trade Center towers.

NATIONAL CONSTITUTION CENTER

Supporters held up signs on a day of a Democratic presidential candidate debate.

COMMITTED TO PUBLIC SERVICE

On Saturday, January 20, 2007, Hillary's friends and supporters received an e-mail from the senator. It said, "I'm in, and I'm in to win."[1] On her Web site, Hillary had posted a video declaring that she had formed a presidential exploratory committee. In the video, which was filmed at her home in Washington DC, she said,

> I'm not just starting a campaign. . . . I'm beginning a conversation—with you, with America. Because we all need to be part of the discussion if we're all going to be part of the solution. And all of us have to be part of the solution. [2]

After announcing her bid for the presidency, Hillary began campaigning in earnest. She took part in several television interviews and also held three days of online video chats. She traveled the country and delivered speeches in which she vowed to restore the economy, reform the government, and create a brighter future for U.S. children.

A HARD-FOUGHT RACE

Early in the primary season, Hillary seemed to be the leading Democratic contender. Because

Female Candidates

Although Hillary came closer than any woman in history to securing the nomination of a major party, she is not the first woman to have run for president. The following women are among the more than 30 candidates of the past:

• In 1870, Victoria Woodhull announced that she was running for president, despite the fact that women did not yet have the right to vote.

• Margaret Chase Smith mounted the first feasible candidacy by a woman in 1964 but lost the Republican nomination to Barry Goldwater.

• In 1972, Shirley Chisholm became the first African-American woman to run for president from a major party.

• Carol Moseley Braun ran for the 2004 Democratic presidential nomination. She ended her campaign due to lack of voter and financial support.

2008 Democratic Candidates

Although Hillary Clinton and Barack Obama were the front-runners during the 2008 Democratic primary season, several others sought the nomination, including:

• John Edwards, former U.S. senator
• Joe Biden, U.S. senator (later chosen as vice president under Barack Obama)
• Chris Dodd, U.S. senator
• Mike Gravel, former U.S. senator
• Dennis Kucinich, U.S. representative
• Bill Richardson, governor of New Mexico

of this, her strategy was to avoid harsh criticism of her Democratic opponents and direct her attacks toward Republican candidates. As the campaign began to intensify, however, she faced stronger criticism from her Democratic rivals and shifted her strategy. Playing on the fact that her leading opponent, Senator Barack Obama of Illinois, had been in the Senate for less than three years, Hillary stressed that she was the only candidate experienced enough to lead the country.

On January 3, 2008, the official process of selecting a Democratic candidate began with the Iowa caucus. In a caucus or a primary, delegates are awarded to candidates. Each state has a specific number of delegates to award based on its population. In Iowa, Hillary came in third with 29 delegates. Obama won 38 delegates, and former Senator John Edwards won 30. In order to secure the

Democratic Party's nomination, a total of 2,118 delegates were needed. The primary race continued as caucuses and primary elections were held across the country in the following months.

Although Hillary won the next three contests— New Hampshire, Michigan, and Nevada—she ultimately was not able to win enough delegates to secure the Democratic nomination. On June 3, 2008, Obama declared that he had surpassed the number of delegates needed, making him the first African American to be nominated as a presidential candidate by a major party. Four days later, Hillary officially ended her

A Family Campaign

Hillary's campaign for president was a family affair, as both Bill and Chelsea often campaigned on her behalf. As a former president, Bill played a unique role in the campaign. He rallied his supporters behind his wife and attended campaign events and fund-raisers around the country. When they traveled together, he often introduced his wife at events. Some people saw Bill as an asset to the campaign, as he used his connections to raise significant sums of money. Others thought he was a detriment because he could overshadow his wife at times.

Chelsea's job on the campaign trail was to win over young voters. The 28-year-old took a leave of absence from her job to travel to college campuses around the country. She answered students' questions about Hillary's views on the issues and talked about the candidate as a mother. Ultimately, Chelsea said of her mom, "There's nobody who I like more and trust more in the entire world."[3]

bid for the presidency. She delivered a concession speech in Washington DC, telling her supporters,

> *The way to continue our fight now, to accomplish the goals for which we stand is to take our energy, our passion, our strength, and do all we can to help elect Barack Obama the next president of the United States.* [4]

In August, Hillary gave a speech at the Democratic National Convention. She called on Democrats to unite behind Obama to defeat his Republican rival, Senator John McCain. They did just that, and in November, Barack Obama was elected the forty-fourth president of the United States.

Secretary of State

Less than one month after Obama's election as president, he announced that he had nominated Hillary to serve as secretary of state

Sexism on the Campaign Trail

Many of Hillary's supporters contend that during her presidential campaign she faced unfair treatment because she was a woman. At one campaign event, for example, hecklers tried to disrupt Hillary's speech by making comments about having her iron their shirts. Hillary's hairstyles and her ankles also became subjects of discussion, and even her cleavage was written about in the *Washington Post*. As a result of such treatment, Howard Dean, the chairman of the Democratic Party, called for a nationwide discussion of sexism.

On January 22, 2009, U.S. State Department employees welcomed the new secretary of state, Hillary Clinton.

in his administration. Many people felt that Hillary was the ideal person for the job. During her time as First Lady, she had traveled the world and established important foreign ties. At the Senate Foreign

Relations Committee hearing to
confirm her appointment, Senator
John Kerry praised Hillary. He said,

> *She will take office on a first-name basis
> with numerous heads of state, but also
> with billions of people in every corner
> of the globe, those billions of people
> that the Obama administration hopes
> to reach, inspire, and influence. Her
> presence will send a strong signal
> immediately that America is back.*[5]

During the hearing on January
13, 2009, Hillary said that her goals
as secretary of state would be to keep
the country and its allies safe, to
promote economic growth in the
United States and around the world,
and to renew the United States'
position as a leader. She pledged to
work with Obama to end the war in
Iraq, to reduce worldwide stockpiles
of nuclear weapons, to address
the problem of terrorism, and to
strengthen U.S. alliances. After her

Silencing Her Critics

When Obama selected
Hillary for secretary of
state, many questioned
whether she would be
able to follow the presi-
dent's lead instead of
directing the course
herself. But after three
months in her role, she
had silenced some of the
skeptics. In April 2009,
the Associated Press
wrote,

"So far Clinton not only
has stayed in sync with
the president's agenda,
she has ceded the public
spotlight on some issues
to designated diplomats.
And inside the White
House, Obama aides say
she has taken care to offer
well-prepared advice
without any of the fric-
tion that some had feared
she would bring. . . .
Presidential aides say the
former first lady is seen
as an effective cham-
pion of Obama's foreign
policy priorities and is a
regular inside the White
House."[6]

testimony, the committee voted to recommend Hillary's nomination to the full Senate, which approved the appointment on January 21, 2009. She resigned her Senate seat and was sworn in as secretary of state that same day.

Within her first days in office, Hillary had placed calls to dozens of foreign leaders and issued a statement about pursuing diplomacy with Iran, an idea that had been out of the question under George W. Bush. In February 2009, she embarked on her first trip overseas as secretary of state. The trip was intended to be a listening tour, much like the one she employed nearly a decade earlier during her first run for the U.S. Senate. Stopping in China, Indonesia, South Korea, and Japan, Hillary announced that the United States was ready to listen to the views of the rest of the world and engage in diplomatic talks.

Traveling Secretary

Traveling to foreign countries and meeting with other nations' leaders is an important function of secretary of state. By the end of April 2009, Hillary had visited 22 countries and logged more than 74,000 airplane miles. Her total travel time was 157 hours and 17 minutes.

As she immersed herself in this new phase of her life, Hillary expressed her continued belief in the nation she had served so long:

> *This is a challenging and defining moment. But I will always keep faith . . . in my fellow Americans. And I remain an optimist that America's best days are still ahead of us.*[7]

As secretary of state, Hillary met with Indonesian President Susilo Bambang Yudhoyono in February 2009.

TIMELINE

1947

Hillary Diane Rodham
is born on October 26
in Chicago, Illinois.

1961

Hillary hears Martin
Luther King Jr.
speak in Chicago.

1965

Hillary graduates
from high school in
Park Ridge, Illinois.

1976

Hillary accepts a
job with the Rose
Law Firm in Little
Rock, Arkansas.

1978

On November 7, Bill
Clinton is elected
governor of Arkansas.

1979

Hillary is made
a partner at the
Rose Law Firm.

1969

On May 31, Hillary graduates from Wellesley College with a degree in political science.

1973

Hillary graduates from Yale Law School.

1975

Hillary marries Bill Clinton on October 11.

1980

The Clintons' daughter, Chelsea, is born on February 27.

1992

On November 3, Bill is elected president of the United States; Hillary becomes First Lady.

1993

On January 25, Bill announces that Hillary will chair the President's Task Force on National Health Care Reform.

TIMELINE

1995	1996	1996
In China, Hillary speaks at the United Nations Fourth World Conference on Women.	On January 26, Hillary testifies before a grand jury in regard to the Whitewater investigation.	On November 5, Bill is elected to a second term as president.

2001	2002	2006
After the 9/11 attacks, Hillary focuses on getting aid to her constituents in New York City.	On October 11, Hillary votes to support the Iraq War.	Hillary is reelected to the Senate on November 7.

1998

On December 19, the U.S. House of Representatives votes to impeach Bill Clinton.

1999

On February 12, Bill is acquitted by the Senate.

2000

On November 7, Hillary is elected to the U.S. Senate.

2007

On January 20, Hillary announces she will run for president.

2008

On June 7, Hillary ends her presidential campaign when Obama exceeds the number of delegates needed to win the Democratic primary.

2009

On January 21, Hillary is sworn in as secretary of state.

ESSENTIAL FACTS

DATE OF BIRTH

October 26, 1947

PLACE OF BIRTH

Chicago, Illinois

PARENTS

Hugh and Dorothy Rodham

EDUCATION

Maine East and South High Schools, Park Ridge, Illinois; Wellesley College, Wellesley, Massachusetts; Yale Law School, New Haven, Connecticut

MARRIAGE

Bill Clinton (October 11, 1975)

CHILDREN

Chelsea

RESIDENCES

Chicago and Park Ridge, Illinois; Wellesley and Cambridge, Massachusetts; New Haven, Connecticut; Fayetteville and Little Rock, Arkansas; Washington DC; Chappaqua, New York

Career Highlights

❖ Served as First Lady, working on health care reform and issues affecting women, children, and families, 1993–2001

❖ Served as a U.S. senator from New York, 2001–2009

❖ Ran for president, 2007–2008

❖ Appointed secretary of state, 2009

Societal Contributions

❖ As First Lady, she spoke out about human rights and women's, children's, and family issues at home and around the world.

❖ As a senator for New York at the time of the September 11, 2001, attacks, she secured funds for New York City's recovery effort.

❖ Hillary's close race for the Democratic presidential nomination helped pave the way for women who will run in the future.

Conflicts

❖ Hillary was often criticized for taking an active role in her husband's governorship and presidency.

❖ In her personal life, Hillary had to face the painful realization that her husband had an affair with a White House intern. She ultimately forgave him, and the two remained together.

Quote

"I have an old-fashioned conviction: that public service is about helping people solve their problems and live their dreams. I've had every opportunity and blessing in my own life, and I want the same for all Americans. Until that day comes, you will always find me on the front lines of democracy—fighting for the future."—*Hillary Rodham Clinton, June 7, 2008*

ADDITIONAL RESOURCES

SELECT BIBLIOGRAPHY

Bernstein, Carl. *A Woman in Charge: The Life of Hillary Rodham Clinton*. New York: Alfred A. Knopf, 2007.

Clinton, Hillary Rodham. *Living History*. New York: Simon & Schuster, 2003.

Osborne, Claire G., ed. *The Unique Voice of Hillary Rodham Clinton: A Portrait in Her Own Words*. New York: Avon Books, 1997.

FURTHER READING

Anderson, Janet. *The Senate*. New York: Chelsea House Publishers, 2007.

Barber, James. *First Ladies*. New York: DK Publishing, 2009.

Ford, Lynne E. *Encyclopedia of Women and American Politics*. New York: Facts on File, 2008.

WEB LINKS

To learn more about Hillary Rodham Clinton, visit ABDO Publishing Company online at **www.abdopublishing.com**. Web sites about Hillary Rodham Clinton are featured on our Book Links page. These links are routinely monitored and updated to provide the most current information available.

Places to Visit

U.S. Capitol
U.S. Capitol Building
Washington, DC 20510
202-226-8000
www.visitthecapitol.gov
The U.S. Capitol is where Congress meets. The Capitol Visitor
Center is open from Monday through Saturday. It is located
beneath the historic Capitol building and contains exhibits about
the House and the Senate as well as about the Capitol building
itself. Tours of the historic Capitol are available by reservation.

U.S. Diplomacy Center
2100 Pennsylvania Avenue NW, Suite 535
Washington, DC 20037
202-736-9040
diplomacy.state.gov/
The U.S. Diplomacy Center features exhibits and educational
programs aimed at teaching the public about the history and
role of U.S. diplomacy. Areas of special interest include a hall
displaying artifacts from the State Department and an exhibition
of condolences received from other countries after the events of
September 11, 2001.

The White House
1600 Pennsylvania Avenue Northwest
Washington, DC 20500
202-456-1414
www.whitehouse.gov/about/tours_and_events
The White House served as the home and office of Bill and Hillary
Clinton from 1993 until 2001. The White House Visitor Center,
which contains information about the mansion's furnishings and
the families who have lived there, is open daily. Appointments are
required for White House tours.

GLOSSARY

acquit
　　To declare a person innocent of a specific charge.

boycott
　　To refuse to buy, use, or deal with a product, a person, or an organization as a form of protest.

caucus
　　A meeting of people from a specific political party to choose delegates or a candidate.

civil rights
　　Rights that all citizens share, such as the right to vote; the civil rights movement focused on securing civil rights for African Americans.

convention
　　A meeting of a political party to nominate a candidate to represent the party in an election.

delegate
　　A representative at a political convention who selects a candidate on behalf of the public.

diplomacy
　　The practice of maintaining international relations through negotiations, alliances, and treaties.

exploratory committee
　　A committee formed to research the feasibility of a campaign for public office.

grand jury
　　A jury that examines evidence against a person accused of a crime to determine whether the case should go to trial.

gubernatorial
　　Relating to a governor.

impeach
> To bring charges against a government official.

inauguration
> A ceremony held for the swearing-in of a public official.

legislation
> The laws made by a ruling body, such as the U.S. Senate.

mediator
> Someone who tries to bring disputing parties into agreement.

nomination
> The selection of a person for a specific position or office.

obstruction of justice
> A crime in which the offender blocks the legal process.

perjury
> Intentionally lying under oath.

polarizing
> Breaking groups or people apart.

primary
> An election in which candidates are chosen to represent their political party in a general election.

segregation
> The separation of groups of people on the basis of race, ethnicity, gender, or other factors.

universal health care
> A health care plan in which the government ensures that all people are provided with health care coverage.

SOURCE NOTES

Chapter 1. First for a First Lady

1. Hillary Clinton. "Keynote Address and Town Hall Meeting At Plenary Session of Foreign Affairs Day." *U.S. Department of State*. 1 May 2009. 8 May 2009 <http://www.state.gov/secretary/rm/2009a/05/122534.htm>.

2. Ana Marie Cox. "How Americans View Hillary: Popular but Polarizing." *Time*. 19 Aug. 2006. 20 Jan. 2009 <http://www.time.com/time/magazine/article/0,9171,1229053,00.html>.

3. "Transcript: Hillary Clinton Speaks in Washington, D.C." *Forbes.com*. 7 June 2008. 19 Jan. 2009 <http://www.forbes.com/2008/06/07/clinton-speech-transcript-oped-cx_hc_0607clintondropsout.html>.

Chapter 2. An Early Love of Politics

1. Hillary Rodham Clinton. *Living History*. New York: Simon & Schuster, 2003. 11.

2. Ibid. 24.

3. Ibid. 22–23.

Chapter 3. Woman of Wellesley

1. Carl Bernstein. *A Woman in Charge: The Life of Hillary Rodham Clinton*. New York: Alfred A. Knopf, 2007. 41.

2. Ibid. 49.

3. Ibid. 54.

4. Hillary Rodham Clinton. *Living History*. New York: Simon & Schuster, 2003. 37.

5. Hillary Rodham. "1969 Student Commencement Speech." *Wellesley College Commencement*. 31 May 1969. 17 Jan. 2009 <http://www.wellesley.edu/PublicAffairs/Commencement/1969/053169hillary.html>.

Chapter 4. Studying the Law

1. Hillary Rodham Clinton. *Living History*. New York: Simon & Schuster, 2003. 38.

2. Carl Bernstein. *A Woman in Charge: The Life of Hillary Rodham Clinton*. New York: Alfred A. Knopf, 2007. 74.

3. Hillary Rodham Clinton. *Living History*. New York: Simon & Schuster, 2003. 52.

4. Ibid. 66.

5. Ibid. 66.

Chapter 5. Moving South

1. Claire G. Osborne, ed. *The Unique Voice of Hillary Rodham Clinton: A Portrait in Her Own Words*. New York: Avon Books, 1997. 16.

2. Hillary Rodham Clinton. *Living History*. New York: Simon & Schuster, 2003. 74.

3. Claire G. Osborne, ed. *The Unique Voice of Hillary Rodham Clinton: A Portrait in Her Own Words*. New York: Avon Books, 1997. 20.

4. Hillary Rodham Clinton. *Living History*. New York: Simon & Schuster, 2003. 84.

5. Hillary Rodham Clinton. *It Takes a Village: And Other Lessons Children Teach Us*. New York: Simon & Schuster, 1996. 9.

6. Carl Bernstein. *A Woman in Charge: The Life of Hillary Rodham Clinton*. New York: Alfred A. Knopf, 2007. 167.

7. Ibid. 171.

8. Ibid. 213.

SOURCE NOTES CONTINUED

Chapter 6. Redefining the First Lady

1. Hillary Rodham Clinton. *Living History*. New York: Simon & Schuster, 2003. 109.
2. Ibid. 125.
3. Ibid. 119.
4. Margaret Carlson Washington. "At the Center of POWER." *Time*. 10 May 1993. 19 Jan. 2009 <http://www.time.com/time/magazine/article/0,9171,978435-4,00.html>.
5. Bill Clinton. *My Life*. New York: Alfred A. Knopf, 2004. 482.
6. Carl Bernstein. *A Woman in Charge: The Life of Hillary Rodham Clinton*. New York: Alfred A. Knopf, 2007. 476.
7. Hillary Rodham Clinton. "Remarks to the U.N. 4th World Conference on Women Plenary Session." *American Rhetoric*. 5 Sep. 1995. 17 Jan. 2009 <http://www.americanrhetoric.com/speeches/hillaryclintonbeijingspeech.htm>.
8. "Mrs. Clinton's Unwavering Words." *New York Times*. 6 Sep. 1995. 9 Feb. 2009 <http://query.nytimes.com/gst/fullpage.html?res=990CE7D81539F935A3575AC0A963958260&scp=1&sq=hillary+clinton+finest+moment&st=nyt>.

Chapter 7. Personal and Public Trials

1. "First Lady Hillary Rodham Clinton Speaks at the Democratic National Convention." *PBS Online NewsHour: Convention Speeches*. 27 Aug. 1997. 19 Jan. 2009 <http://www.pbs.org/newshour/convention96/floor_speeches/hillary_clinton.html>.
2. Hillary Rodham Clinton. *Living History*. New York: Simon & Schuster, 2003. 393.
3. "First Lady Hillary Rodham Clinton Speaks at the Democratic National Convention." *PBS Online NewsHour: Convention Speeches*. 27 Aug. 1997. 19 Jan. 2009 <http://www.pbs.org/newshour/convention96/floor_speeches/hillary_clinton.html>.
4. Hillary Rodham Clinton. *Living History*. New York: Simon & Schuster, 2003. 471.

Chapter 8. Senator Clinton

1. Hillary Rodham Clinton. *Living History.* New York: Simon & Schuster, 2003. xi.

2. Hillary Rodham Clinton. "Senate Floor Speech: Authorization of the Use of United States Armed Forces Against Iraq." *Political Library.* 10 Oct. 2002. 7 Feb. 2009 <http://politicallibrary.net/library/C/Clinton%20Hillary/clinton_h_senate_2002_10_10.htm>.

3. Carl Bernstein. *A Woman in Charge: The Life of Hillary Rodham Clinton.* New York: Alfred A. Knopf, 2007. 36.

Chapter 9. Committed to Public Service

1. Jeff Gerth and Don Van Natta, Jr. *Her Way: The Hopes and Ambitions of Hillary Rodham Clinton.* New York: Little, Brown and Company, 2007.

2. "Clinton Takes Step Toward 2008 Bid." Washingtonpost.com. 21 Jan. 2007. Online video clip. 7 Feb. 2009. <http://www.washingtonpost.com/wp-dyn/content/article/2007/01/20/AR2007012000426.html>.

3. Arian Campo-Flores. "Chelsea Come Lately." *Newsweek.* 18 Feb. 2008. 17 Jan. 2009 <http://www.newsweek.com/id/109592>.

4. "Transcript: Hillary Clinton Endorses Barack Obama." *New York Times.* 7 June 2008. 19 Jan 2009 <http://www.nytimes.com/2008/06/07/us/politics/07text-clinton.html>.

5. "Sen. John Kerry Holds a Hearing on the Nomination of Sen. Hillary Rodham Clinton to Be Secretary of State." FDCH Political Transcripts. 13 Jan. 2009. EBSCOHost. Web. 17 Jan. 2009.

6. Robert Burns. "Analysis: Clinton Making No Waves As Top Diplomat." *Boston Globe Online.* 21 Apr. 2009. 22 Apr. 2009 <http://www.boston.com/news/nation/washington/articles/2009/04/22/analysis_clinton_making_no_waves_as_top_diplomat/?page=1>

7. "Clinton's Senate Farewell Speech" *RealClearPolitics.* 15 Jan. 2009. 9 Feb 2009 <http://www.realclearpolitics.com/articles/2009/01/clintons_senate_farewell_speec.html>.

INDEX

ABOUT THE AUTHOR

Valerie Bodden is a freelance author and editor. She has written nearly 100 children's nonfiction books. Her books have received positive reviews from *School Library Journal*, *Booklist*, *ForeWord Magazine*, *Horn Book Guide*, *VOYA*, and *Library Media Connection*. Bodden lives in Wisconsin with her husband and their two children.

PHOTO CREDITS

Charles Dharapak/AP Images, cover, 6; Kevin Wolf/AP Images, 8, 91; Alex Brandon/AP Images, 13; Paul Beaty/AP Images, 14; AP Images, 20, 23, 24, 53; Sygma/Corbis, 27; Time & Life Pictures/ Getty Images, 33; Bob Child/AP Images, 34; William J. Clinton Presidential Library, Clinton Family Photographs, 38; Charlie Harrity/AP Images, 43; Fayetteville Advertising and Promotion Commission, 44; Barry Thumma/AP Images, 49; Donald R. Broyles/AP Images, 51; Craig Fuji/AP Images, 54; Stephen R. Brown/AP Images, 59; Greg Baker/AP Images, 62; Denis Paquin/ AP Images, 65; Rick Bowmer/AP Images, 66; Karin Cooper/AP Images, 70; J. Scott Applewhite/AP Images, 75; Kathy Willens/ AP Images, 76; Jim McKnight/AP Images, 79; Mark Lennihan/ AP Images, 85; Carolyn Kaster/AP Images, 86; Mast Irham/AP Images, 95